Peter Br[illegible]

TORCH OF VENUS

a narrative

To Simon –
With warmest regards –
Peter Brennan

30.iii.'10

PERDIKA EDITIONS 5

PERDIKA EDITIONS 5
Series Editors: Peter Brennan,
Mario Petrucci & Nicholas Potamitis

Published by Perdika Press
2007

Perdika Press
16B St. Andrew's Road
Enfield MIDDX
EN1 3UB UK

www.perdikapress.com

Set by N. Potamitis in Monotype Joanna

ISBN: 978-1-905649-04-4

Acknowledgements

My warmest thanks to Mario, for his unstinting care and support for this project, and to Nick for his belief and encouragement.

An audiofile of the sequence may be heard at www.archiveofthenow.com. 'Venus Again' appears in the anthology *Into the Further Reaches* (PS Avalon).

"You stood before me like a thought."

Coleridge

Torch of Venus

– for Alison – across the lifetimes –

Just now I thought
to dream again

that blinded
night when

despair of you
rode over me

it went where

these things go
– the adored

face wearing
its years

the needs that visit
your tower

as once more
they visit mine

Venus Again

She sits serene
above the loft
conversions opposite

moving unflustered down the weeks
at an unvarying
height.

Not to be mistaken
for an aircraft or
a satellite.

Herself
in truth,
soliciting

no tribute from the street
where her unblinking light
declines

the self
-referring night. Her fragrant
lips encompassing

fulness of desire – as we
in dream of ending
abdicate.

Her eye
unflinching
offers end

-lessness. Watching the mate
who watches close the
one he'd make his own –

dares him to warm
his heart at her cool pale
fire, her cloudy throne.

1

Birdsong
scours the morning

crouches in branches

peers through dreams.

Leaves are splattered
ink against
the creamy blue, neutral

wash of sunrise.

You
elsewhere, sated, tousled,
celluloid dreaming
flickering lids. Arms
stretching, re
compose.

I
elsewhere, awake
between walls. Hearing
birds declaim
life's details,
wary daylight's
subterfuge.

2

Walls
engulfing a crepuscular
world. Your friend
dead before life
had spoken.

A painting –
you.
Naked with symbols. Dis
posed, un
nerved,
arrogating time,
                    queenliness.

                    Venus
emerging
foam-flecked,
magnetising
the newformed realm

where scythes and sickles
arc and reap,
send abundance
down to hell.

3 *Intervals: in absentia*

I

Five Wordsworthian years
stretch in between.
In bower and bed you
speculate. Test
promises. Broke,
mostly.

Silken fingers
soothe the daybreak.

II

Flight. Violent aspiration
of Apennine and Alp
flash back in the glacial mirror
fierce Augustan light.

III

Roman cloisters
disclose the woman. A dress
pays homage, heels high

a camera lens
insists
on beauty, probes
the folds
of womb, opening

4

Flight.

One Saturday
where Eliot and Heathcliff had deposed
brown eyes
sparked up at me, laughing eager
words con
founded me. Remembrance

from behind
a screen invited
journeys,
couplings.

To contemplate again
the face
lost a dozen
lives ago when

a bird
flickered easily
as returning vows

and the day
defined its potency.

In Orphean glades
of morning – you and I

aligned.

5

In Arabian dawns
Sufi flutes

rasp. On divans where

you taught me
how a girl's
way enslaves

the driver, turns to
rubies every
lash.
Hear a Sultan

groan
as he awaits
the tinkling

feet, the
slender
thoughtless

form emerge beyond
the fretwork's last
enticing.

And what bleak partings
then, those wintry
sunsets?

A
kiss, a touch, a glance of
intrigue, knowing
the wheel would bring us

back to wander by
this placid lake,

and in the dunes
to know again
the landscape
of the heart,

reconstitute our
outcast part
in this
great circling

confluence of
all that ever has
been and will be
to make this simple
now.

6

A pool
green with the duckweed
of a summer's childhood.
Mossy trees. Rushes. A bicycle
almost forgotten in
the long grass fringing
carillon bluebells.

From the cauldron deep
beneath the morning's aquamarine
a crone arises and before
dismay and terror

overtake the boy,
a lilting
            maiden to caress
his ancient fears:

"Do not deplore
your destiny, for look,

"beside your anguish
I have sent you
this my daughter, in whose arms
the wise themselves
are pleased to be
entwined."

7 *Cambridge*

Even to King's Cross booking-hall
sunrays filter inevitably down.

We choose the train that sways
and curves by Stort and Lea, glinting
words from lip to lip
– remembrances,
learnings of the week –
patterns gingerly
unpicked. As if each birth were
but a sampler
balanced on a maiden's knee.

Champagne among the indoor
fronds and palms –
down King's Parade I buy
for you a disc
of tsifteteli's
poised and lilting
integral narcosis.

Returning, the world
revives, and is with us – upstaging
the harem trance the clarified
self with vulgar,
Monday-charged anxieties.

We know, though, where
we were. Not now,
but it had been, and briefly
of all we imaged to create
we were its king and queen.

8

“We scrub up well!” you chimed –
a princess, hair pinned
high and ringlets
drawing down the glance

to creamery of neck and
shoulders, slender

arms (whose cool soft mallow
intoxicates the fingertips’ fine webbery
of fascinated nerves) – a dress the sheen of

silver and night, breasts
distinctly poised and
etched.

Riding the opera house
escalator, in pride beside
you, rising to
the gods –
Your Italy had come to me
as you had gone to it to melt
the ice around your heart.

We named each myth
before and after
it was sung.

Scenes revealed
sapphires of understanding –

the court of
cruel extinction, barbarous
death – passing the scimitar –
the revenge of sex;

made soberly and
glad our journey back.

And when I next looked in
the simple screen,
I clicked on each
attachment disbelievingly –

concavities con
vexities becoming
you in maiden pride

the outline of
the thought of God
transfigured now
as subtle play's

persisting dream, where
days elide and all is
as the form
would have it
seem.

9

Birthdays at the heart of the sun.
Solstices at which you worshipped.
In the garden, in blue,
you painted
beauty in that rosy
book of ours.

(The sun that saw a slender
goddess – turned aside
wearing only
heart-shaped leaves –
eloquently grace my wall).

Elsewhere from
another frame
you look direct on
those who seek you there.
But here – though averted
that adamant gypsyfire

your white
curves languidly
entice the halting
heart to brakes unknown

to see unseen
as gods, our only company.

10

There were just those days
we'd meet and walk
by withy bed and open mere

or talk in Starbucks
and be friends and
always the old story

to know again

11

I closed
the curtains. You
swiftly

unclasped

their
white completeness

soon contained again,

my gaze become
a lifetime's
slivered glass.

So many mornings
have woken from that moment

"If only
you'd taken me

by the shoulders and said
you loved me."

12

We go as one
through gaudy streets
leaning in to anchor, the
familiar pulse
shaping and shading
the world's bewildering.

To the casbah the souk
dancer and warrior
envining and severing –
arabesques in a table of brass

spice sacks compact
with brick coloured dust,
musky unfurling
intimacy

   ...we part as always
we part. The golden hours
flake to the wind, the
destinies
insist –

some prior under
standing – some hope

less edict countermanding

every law of life.

13

I am
the one who knew
you at dawn in
the fortress at eve in
the temple at night in
the sacred wood
                    Look there
is your star there
mine sometimes

they keep their
spheres alway

                    I am your
paramour in Attic
groves
                    they find
us and would
humble our
adultery

14 *The Garden*

The reading you
had sought to defuse

(tumbling frames of berries
and a fragrant
August sun).

With each
tribute, you
toyed with your

bikini top –
accepting homage
awkwardly

declining the fruit
scrupulously

(as the perfect afternoon looked on
no blackbird caught its breath

the Voice spoke mildly
in the heat of the day

the animals snuffled
content with their names)

and we – walked back
untouching

and most free

15

"No more," you said, "no more
for me of this."

You took the song but sent
the singer

slowly
away

            gently

eased my grip upon
the faded covers

and through the shark blue darkness
drove me

                        quietly home